THE BLAMELESS LIFE

POEMS BY
ADRIAN BUCKNER

PUBLISHED BY THE NOTTINGHAM POETRY SOCIETY
1997

Poems © Adrian Buckner

ISBN - 0   906842 12 3

Poetry Nottingham Poets: New Series No. 8

Series Editor: Cathy Grindrod

Typeset and Printed by
Christian Duplicating Service, 3 Castle Road, Nottingham, NG1 6AA.

CONTENTS

Acknowledgments
to

IOTA
LONDON MAGAZINE
POETRY NOTTINGHAM INTERNATIONAL
ORBIS
STAPLE
THE FROGMORE PAPERS
WORKING TITLES

PERSPECTIVE

She is between times on the clock
With her child by the wooden swing.
A brief sojourn, extended by the visible haze
And a single dawdling man in a wide space.
An unthreatening dog,
A well mannered old gent
Pass.
Vigilance can evaporate into the sun
In a thoughtless tranquillity,
A serene half hour between ease and boredom.

Half a pound of butter begins to melt
On warm gravel in a plastic carrier bag.
Her husband is home at five.

On this hot afternoon
The light is everlasting
On infant skin.
A long day, the morning beyond memory
In a vast tactile world -
Soaring to heaven
In this gigantic garden
Under Mother's eye.

His dad returns when the day is old
At the beginning of the never ending dark.

THE ANCIENT SUNBATHER

He's not impressed by warnings
of a hole in the sky:

Six weeks and not a drop of rain;
he is back in a golden age

of summers possessed undimmed
in his ageing heart.

He lies in the parched land
like a die hard colonist

sticking it out in Delhi after '47,
making a go of the new Rhodesia -

unmoved by forebodings of a world
falling in, a setting sun.

A VILLAGE CRICKETER CONSIDERS HIMSELF

Here I stand, midwicket saving one,
though I am rather more attached

to my grander and recently
re-acquired status of cultural icon -

it keeps my mind off that nostril pierced
daughter of mine and her friends;

helps me forget the mortgage, the meeting
on Monday, that bloody gearbox.

All things considered I would rather
be viewed as a white eternal spirit

forever walking in with the bowlers of England
across one boundless village ground

than to be seen and heard
living this life I live.

And if all this sounds as outlandish
as a Prime Minister's election stunt

let me at least be seen today
from a passing express train

about to execute the perfect cover drive,
orientating myself composedly under the the highest skier,

becoming a split second enigma for those
who, slumped and gazing through glass,

discover that England has occurred to them.

After Major, after Orwell

BLOOD DONOR HEAVEN

The queue is five rows deep - we shift passively
seat by seat - no, no, as far as I know, no.

Yes, I'm feeling well today - just the normal
checkup - no, no, as far as I know, no.

This bed please. Buckner, 18th of the 7th, 62.
That's lovely - would you like the anaesthetic?

Another one? Already mantra-drugged I lie
back, loving the idea of it not hurting.

Plenty in today. Yes, Christmas brings you all out -
busy this morning too? Oh Splendid!

Someone's feeling a little faint - O.K. now? Yes.
How easy, how painless, this doing the right thing.

Just the five minutes rest today? Make sure
you get your cup of tea. I want to stay for ever.

I dream through it - muzak and whitewashed
ceiling; no, no, as far as I know, no.

Left to my own devices now - digestive or
custard cream? Tea, coffee or chocolate?

Bringing me back gently to the world of
decisions and self reliance - but I'd rather stay
                 the Blood Donor Centre
this afternoon at Castle Boulevard Blood
Donor Centre, Nottingham because in truth
         Castle Bonlevard, Nottingham, because in truth
I've never really wanted to stand on my own
two feet; no, no, as far as I can remember, never.

8

ON READING THE TRACTS OF THOMAS PAINE

I may protest, admit it with a hesitation
But reading is for me a spare time recreation:
I want no esoteric doctrines from which to choose,
Only articles in newspapers that confirm my views -
To read in bed and put out the light
Not staggered by the pen and its might;
Poems brief and lucid fit the bill,
Not a liberty treatise by J.S. Mill.
So Paine, you gave me much of the same
With your tracts so mighty glorious and plain -
All my responses were out of joint,
I seemed to wilfully miss the point
For Nations, Liberty and Fraternal dreams
Just don't fit in with my reading scheme:
With "Common Sense" you galvanized a nation,
I read it three mornings at a railway station;
"The Crisis" fired Washington's weary men -
I got the gist over tea at ten;
Your reply to Burke slipped before my eyes
One dead afternoon between four and five.
In your Republic's literary court "The Rights of Man"
Would demand justice for so trivial a scan
So I'd best attend to this High Treason
Before I tackle "The Age of Reason".

SUBURBAN MEMORY

It was the kind of afternoon
When the garden needs the rain.

When you look at the lawn's deep green
And the red brick of next door's back;

Learn from a T.V. documentary
How a cricket ball is stitched.

The kind of afternoon when only
The old are at home and stay indoors

Watching folk pass through the net curtains,
Make tea for one and water the plants.

It was the kind of day
That slows down after half past one

With reposeful thoughts of
A husband passed on, a son up north;

The kind of afternoon I only took one sweet
And never forgot to say thank you

For the home made jam and gardening hint
I'd always take home to Mother.

SUPERVISING TEACHER, WITH COFFEE MUG

A love from afar, I'd gaze from all corners
of the yard they spilled us out to;

a love puré, demanding no requital
no touch, just a wide visual embrace

that included me, aged eight, otherwise roaming
shy and bored from ten thirty to forty five;

a love unspecified - he or she, hard or
indulgent, head teacher or graduate student.

It was the poise and easy benevolence
that enraptured me - I never suspected

they'd rather be inside or resented
being conned into another shift.

For me they couldn't possibly not love it,
stood there like domesticated royalty, musing

unpestered on the even greater buzz to be had
writing in red across thirty English Compositions.

Once I got near enough, brave enough to ask
Mrs Harley what she did after half past three

and when she said she had a home much
like mine, shopped at Tesco's like my Mum

I didn't believe her, but loved her all the more
for being kind enough to kid me.

Three years on I'd come over misty and
admiring of the first XI's opening bat

but I'm sticking with that old saw -
nothing beats the first time.

DEATH OF A SMALL TALKER

Mornings he would hold court in the library
cheerfully infringing the rule of silence;

after lunch go door to door picking up
newspapers and aluminium cans.

His real business was to accept with grace
all invitations over the threshold -

pay attention to the details of lives
which aimed only at a sedate passing:

He had a heart of gold, was a meddlesome pest,
averaging out at about harmless.

Monday to Friday, mid morning to mid afternoon
he trimmed the verges of a marginal world

and now that he's gone a few quiet lives
have been nudged a little further towards empty. *that way*

MIDWINTER SUN

Slashed and splintered
into each crystal of frost
on the graveyard wall,
singeing the thousand points
of a thousand naked trees.

I strode downhill
from common to marketplace
along a molten trail
daubed across every admired
construct of the city.

On the pond the retreating ice
was chased and mocked
under a sky swept clear
for a harried
late rising sun.

I felt no cold
but a well wrapped cool;
hot tea sunk in my stomach,
the warmth of your body
still in me.

EXECUTED

The alarm was an instant summons
from dreamless sleep
to the awakening moment
of someone else's nightmare.
The words from the clock radio
dropped in appalling order . . .
Reuters . . . journalist . . . hung . . .
Iraq . . . this morning.
The bedroom air choked
and tightened in the throat
as if to join breath
that left a young body.

- *Farzad Bazoft, journalist, murdered by the Iraqi State, March 1990.*

NAKED AGGRESSION

He ploughed fifty lengths
with a flawless stroke
at perfect pace,
goggles navigating
a straight charmless line,
arms cutting water
with surgical precision.

He's never felt better -
fighting fit,
showers and dries himself
hard and fast,
assertively nude.
"We should go in"
he says
"and bomb the hell out of them."

THE BLAMELESS LIFE

Midweek, mid afternoon, mid fifty degrees -
grey but only grey, the cloud

bears no menace above the sparse
community gathered around the pond:

A three year old, amused and undemanding,
her father peering now and then over his broadsheet;

a suited escapee from the half mile
distant city throwing crumbs on the pond

then gazing to the other side where the tramp
exercises his peculiar talent with squirrels;

two park employees pacing the hour, clearing
leaves that have mulched for weeks by the aviary

and the exotic birds, watching, bored and quiet,
accepting this is not a propitious time

like serpents in the first garden, observing
a blameless, undamaged fraction of life.

CELESTIAL

Exploding on the stoic gaze
of a winter's morning queue
a two year old
bundle of chaos
crashing like a nova
through our unmoving cluster
flings one arm skyward
and in a gushing breath
bursting from layers of warm
blurts a dozen heady words
climbing to the final exhilarating STAR!

GROUNDED

Two lovers, one kite -
failing to sustain height
they collapse in a heap
of not caring.
Eighteen months - buttoned and togged
he twists, a chunky spinning top,
arms flung heavenward
urging renewal of flight.
Mother's hardby, feet firmly on the ground,
a slow smile for
two of her disappeared worlds.

THUG

Heads turned on the top deck,
eyes grappled to figure
and organise the intent flash
in which he struck - four blows
clean, honed; an abstract hate
at the flesh encounter -
then strode on, festooned
in red and white,
plundered yellow and green,
resuming his cigarette
as the denuded victim uncurled.

ANTIQUARIAN

I shove the door,
bring down the clatter of bells.
The bookseller sips coffee,
gazing on the road
throwing up its wet circular noise:
Peace, chanced upon like clover
between leaves of Dombey and Son;
Touch, satisfied
by the stiff discoloured flyleaf;
Taste, the scent
of rain on my clothes.   ₃

GIRL ON A COACH

You couldn't find
a vacant pair of seats
but I can't look at you.
I have a vague impression
of your hair abundant,
your thigh touching mine.

I glance at the right-hand page
and see your sunned arm,
tiny golden hairs
which seem to penetrate my shirt.

At journey's end
you are in focus,
lifesize and beautiful;
I pull your bag from the rack,
hand it to you
and fix a chaste smile.

POETRY TEACHER

Class dismissed
he happens in the English cupboard
upon a single unused text
- grammar school stamped
nineteen-fifty-eight-
stuffed with lyrics
prim and square;
there's one or two gems
but they've taken their places
in new styles of packaging,
no need for him to root around here.
Lulled for a moment
he browses two quatrains
back cover bent for imminent doom,
then fans insouciantly
through a thousand more
wafting towards his nose
the musty scent of poems
that have lost all meaning -
it is the smell of death.
Class dismissed.

A MEMORY OF PHIL LAWRENCE, 1980

Now the plaque's unveiled they want you for
their patron saint - the law and order salivators

the thou shalt not alliance; vote for hanging, for
juvenile tagging - vote for you, their Man of the Year:

For loving the decent they took Orwell,
for naked courage they'll take you too.

****

Entering our sixth form class sixteen years ago
you tumbled your unwieldy load on the front desk,

unwound that foppish scarf and standing
on tiptoes, fingertips stretched to the desk

surveyed us mock kingly, out stared the back row
then dissolved with us in laughter.

Philip Lawrence - Headmaster, murdered at his school gates, 1995

20 YEARS DREAMING

He mixed humiliation with merriment -
"one of the old school" was the euphemism;

ordered me into the corner to jog on the spot
for paying insufficient attention to Newfoundland.

"Get your knees up lad! Wake up!
Your chest's in a funny place! Knees up!"

Later, softened, he took me aside:
"Son, you can't dream your life away."

Twenty years on, I'm gazing over the city
from the seventh floor, behind me

office files and cabinets strike home,
a rattle of cutlery down the corridor

and someone's tedious sex joke
getting the standard issue giggle.

Dead afternoon. Dead paper world.
Have all the meetings you want,

nothing of use is happening here -
better to dream your life away

if you've got the staying power.

LAST OUT

Airy and flirtatious they scurry away,
voices dying at a hundred yards

and gone from this space like
an evaporation of summer rain.

Their husbands and lovers stay behind
faithful and upright in brass frames -

smiling in their homes and gardens amid
the ignored memos and paper clips;

sticky backed notes curl from desks,
flutter in an extractor fanned dusk

as a dimmed unfrivolous light settles
at last on the depopulated office.

I trip the switch, bin the plastic cups -
lubricants for every dizzy Friday dream.

PINK WINDOWS

In art class
With cardboard and glue
Lisa, aged seven
Has built her home
Like the committees dreamed it,
Tall in the sunshine
With pink windows

Looking out to
Smiling semi-circle mouths
And deep green grass
Daubed like heavy
Graffiti lines.

And to finish, herself
Labelled in thick blue capitals, ME -
A stylized matchstick girl
With blond curls.

She's dead central:
Innocent still,
Already wise.

FACTORY RETIREMENT

He went with an engraved watch
and a portable T.V. on his hip.
His working life has ended,
a life that did not touch us.
We routinely smoked and joked,
sympathised over his knees
that were weaker than most -
all that goes with him
is our notice of him.

And all he left
lasted one afternoon -
something buttoned, unconsummate
across a few faces,
from which the encircling space
of the loading dock stretched
out through the open shutters,
across the city heights, grieving
for meaning unfound, emotion unattained.

CENTENARY EXHIBITION

Wrapped against winter in a forty year old
black and white, framed in silence

and submission to the maiden aunt behind
the issuing desk - the dark hunched readers

take part in the library's celebration
as earnest hunters of knowledge,

not as the barely tolerated, back exited
each morning by landladies or competent relatives;

in from the street seeking warmth and
a grim, muttering companionship.

Celebration. Nostalgia. Not bad words, just
cheated on, diminished like the shelves.

Outside, the no longer tolerated browse and bark -
going mad the old fashioned way.

ONE LOOK AT HIM

He arrived every morning at eight
from rented rooms that no-one ever saw;
one look at him told you
they'd be a shameful mess.

He drank too much and washed too little;
one look at him and you knew
he just wasn't up to the mark.

He fed pigeons and looked out for stray cats
but that counted for nothing or worse -
he was clearly hopeless with people.

Our courteous words were wasted,
he seemed to stare through any civil address:
We cursed him but he didn't give a damn -
his skin was thick enough.

"He served for thirty six years"
ran the staff obituary column,
"our thoughts are with his aged mother."

4

THE DILETTANTE

To mankind he was in the main, amiably disposed
though generally unmoved to detain them -

"Too beautiful to work all day" he'd say
then ease for an acquaintance passing by

a slow disengaged smile, leaving them
with the sense of not having been invited.

In the sunshine he browsed the broadsheets where
from time to time his reviews appeared,

kept, in cooler weather, his quiet corner
in the City's more convivial pubs and eateries.

He wasn't much taken with attics or basements,
places where scholastic stuff got strewn around.

"A minor talent" ran the obituary column,
"whose early work showed exquisite touch."

Eight hundred words, expanding on a theme -
It had been too beautiful, too often, to work all day.

To mankind, he was in the main
amiably disposed
though generally unmoved / to detain
its representatives

JACK 1905 - 1990

The crematorium wears warm autumn colour
to host our small circle of quietude:
Removed from the priest's exhorting bombast
on God, Country, Family and Work
these are the authentic moments - passed
in undertones and the admiring of flowers,
each thought unguided, unheroic but wise enough
to remember him justly, not a driven
soul but a loved and ordinary man
who in my mind bellows "My darling Clementine"
whilst rub-clapping his hands above the wheel
of the ancient mini, foot tapping
over the hole in the floor.

AN AIRING FOR LOVE

An early evening in summer,
the city edge droops with lassitude
and on the warm public air
a song of lost love
breathes from a high window.
I make out each known by heart word,
learnt in self-regarding youth
when grief was borrowed
and love overstated.
Now the keening female voice
drifts away from spurious profundity;
a simple strain of regret,
a wafted note of loveliness
seeping from a high window
to blend with the plebeian cat,
the clamorous play of children
and the cares of parents
who wearily urge restraint
and wish for gardens.

ALL DAY A BURNING

All day a burning
into the grid of streets:
Fruit ruins in trays at the corner shop
and the gutters deteriorate
to a stretch of takeaway scraps.
Over the heaved out engine of a blue Citroen
three youths consult,
oil blotted like sprayed territory marks;
a pugnacious rattle of Urdu,
a volley of ebullient Nottingham
scything the air of a ragged dusk
that awaits the fresh draught of darkness.
  And the common,
diminished by time and tarmac
yearns against roads
that bind it to town, distils
peace from motortone
and the unhurried gait of those who cross it.
The towerblock is winking neon;
day is closing like the eyes of a cradled child,
graceful extinction unfurls
from the shadows of aged trees.

A HARD HABIT

Most Sundays, weather and his mood permitting,
we sit on this bench from two till nearly four:

I will not say that words are unnecessary after thirty years,
only that when they were most needed I could never find them.

It's so long since his drinking was a problem,
years since he hit me, since my friends insisted I leave;

the weeks between bouts became months then a year
had passed. I think that is what broke me,

the unaccountable tailing off of violence - the fight
was at last rising in me - I am a victim of peace.

I spilt tears of pain and rage - I have not shed one
for years now - there is a flood behind my eyes, cold;

I know that he would tip every one out of me
with one word of remorse, even anger

and that is why I sit here with him, rigid,
the words in my heart unspoken, their argument uncontested.

He is watching young women sunbathe, sometimes
I do the same, remembering that brief cluttered time of joy,

lounging in the corners of this park where he first
planted then nourished in me this ruinous love.

I do not think he is remembering but
you never know, I've not known for so long.

RELEASE

I've been waiting most of the afternoon
to register the bald fact of his death,

smiling occasionally out of respect for the living
toward the young couples and pushchairs opposite;

at least a dozen, processed rapidly at the
starting tape of life have come and gone

whilst I have sat here, back against the high
Victorian wall, browsing across the dark panelling

and breathing in the order imposed on my
calamity by these civil servants of God.

For half an hour my spine stiffened - something
to get through and out of here

- You see I have not been taking it well
have not been bearing up with a brave face

in front of the family and neighbours, most
of whom hold opinions on my past and future -

but when the registrar passed me for the third time
with someone else's document, her standard issue glance

at once both solicitous and disregarding
released me from the sharp end of grief

and closing my eyes I concentrated on
the muted sequence of her footfall, a sound

the like of which I did not think could be heard
amid the screaming clutter in my head.

And a little peace was upon me, from the
rawness of loss, from my comforters ....
away away.

32

REMAINING DETAILS

Her letters were pictures on the finest paper
Signed with a brisk pressure, a mark
Competent, complacent and indecipherable.
Archaically, we took money to her door.

For matters undertaken, transactions underway,
For dealings set in motion, requirements duly met,
We signed here and signed there.
Clipped and functional tones wrapped the business up.

"One or two remaining details
I must draw your attention to -
If anything should happen to either of you ..."

And in the half minute that followed
A few words withered into vagueness
Before death was signed away
Without a flicker across three faces,
For God is in his heaven
And all's well in the best of articled worlds.

MOTHER WAKING CHILD

Stirring under my gaze, you persuade
A pocket of heat from the bedclothes;

You are drenched in the scent of your infant slumber,
Your breath perfumed with the love my body gives;
Your ruffled hair I ruffle a little more
My fingers lingering through the down.

In this unburdened minute all sound
Comes as lullaby within these walls,

I have no thoughts, only a still spirit
No movement save a caressing hand;
Ardent yet becalmed I give to you in the stillness
That which you can never lose and I never retrieve.

You will make one leap into the morning
And I resume my waking to the world.

Stirring under my gaze, you persuade
a pocket of heat from the bedclothes;
You are drenched in the scent of your slumber,
breath perfumed with my body's love.
Your ruffled hair I ruffle a little more,
finger lingering through the down

GONE AWAY

Gone away, you say,
then a worldly shrug
of two year old shoulders.
Gone away, the pigeons
you chase in the park,
the bee that hovers fleetingly
over the unopened chalice
of honeysuckle,
the fair leaving town
this weekend -
You make no distinctions:
Gone away takes them all,
a vast encompassing destination
like the one road
wide and endless in a flat land.
You stand at one end,
all around you
is what your eyes know
·as the land of come back.

ALICE

To grandparents in Columbia
you are a bundle of exotica
loved and unknown
while in your mother's arms
you wake to autumn, England
and her avenue afternoons.

SEPTEMBER

A single leaf
floats down to the grass court,
falling behind her shoulder
as she leans into the final serve -
every year brings the moment,
sweetened yet undiluted.

Mornings of the mind
they never are so dark
as under low September skies
for June is precarious
but late summer, if
once strung out with joy,
endless.

RAIN IN TOWN

Only lazy leakage from tedious sky
to hearts and minds ensnared
behind the panes of city blocks:
Rain with no intent save to dribble
on the flagstones a silky anointment
and revive all afternoon a churchyard rose.

THE SEASON OF DAFFODILS

Three days after knowing the worst
she noticed the first bloom in her garden,

knew then that the season of his dying
would be the season of daffodils:

Each day showed her new abundance
in the town and hospital grounds

but she picked out the single flowers
cut down by winds insane with malice.

He was foul-mouthed, unbroken; the doctors
rational and kind; she'd hear them both out

then gaze outside to the teeming yellow -
all gains were relentless.

When the clusters began to ail
her eyes sought again the individual flowers

ravaged and tossed in a frenzy
of concentration to stay alive.

HUNSTANTON, SEPTEMBER

From the caravan park it's a promenade width
and a leapable wall to the beach.

"I could let you all run free, forget
about you" says my mother, as we sit

on the front's low wall, a quarter century
later, watching the tide retreat and

the beach's diminished end of season population,
unmoved like ourselves by the compulsions of August:

The dawdling or sedentary retired
and young couples with infant children

perched for a hundred yard ride
on the world's slowest donkeys;

engraving their names and "Mummy"
with the cane of a fishing net.

Two figures are dabbling for shells -
he, on his haunches is near seventy,

she, perhaps four, ranges further, running
back to him every excited half minute

with a new contender for the beach's
most gorgeous specimen;

then peering into his upturned palm
at his deliberate and sober offering.

How well-graced they appear, sublime detail
in this widening space I frame -

elementally free; joined with each other,
the sky and sea, about to uncover

like a redeemed promise between the generations
the most beautiful shell on the beach.

NOTES ON A CONTRIBUTOR

A child who kept his head down, forever
reading in the back of the family car -

rarely interested enough to observe the workings
of a wheel, clutch or map,

to watch my elder brother being capable,
getting to places and fixing things up.

My mother shed tears of fear when I
couldn't tie my laces at seven -

hugged me, tears again, when red stars
appeared next to my English compositions.

Somehow, it balanced itself out: "A dream of
delight but such a hoot, a way with words."

At twenty two the road I'd chosen
got blocked off and I never chose another,

just played over and over the aborted journey -
pondered, read and got looked after.

Half the time I fool myself it's been
conversation and ideas that have formed me

for with a comforting delusion you can live
with the truth - the child in the back seat

of the family car, head down and ignoring
the capable, mending and fixing world.